# ALPHA
# THOUGHT

POCKET EDITION

Published from
Mardukite Borsippa HQ, San Luis Valley, Colorado
Mardukite Academy & Systemology Society
*for spiritual or educational purposes only*

# ALPHA THOUGHT

## Systemology Professional Course Booklet #16

Developed by Joshua Free
for the Systemology Society

© 2023, JOSHUA FREE

ISBN : 978-1-961509-41-2

Pocket Paperback Edition — *December 2023*

**mardukite.com**

# Chart Your Flight For Ascension...
## Then Let Your Spirit Fly!

Unlock your ultimate spiritual potential by removing barriers to your true native state.

Learn how to easily attain Self-actualization and help to actualize others along the way.

A greater appreciation and understanding of *Spiritual Life* and *Existence* awaits you. Expand your reach to achieve your dreams.

Each 'Professional Course' lesson-booklet offers simple exercises and techniques that directly apply the philosophy of Systemology, assisting to increase your true knowingness, improve your capabilities in this life, and even decide what you will do in your next.

At the Mardukite Academy of Systemology, the 'Professional Course' lessons in this series are presented to Seeker's that have already completed the 'Basic Course', previously released as six lesson-booklets, or the six-in-one single volume edition "Fundamentals of Systemology."

This all new presentation of the Systemology 'Pathway-to-Ascension' takes Seekers and continuing students from "Zero" to "Infinity" at lightning-fast speeds!

## Discover Who You Really Are...

## Because You Were Never Human

## <u>Fundamentals of Systemology</u>
### Basic Course Lesson Booklet Series

## <u>The Pathway to Ascension</u>
### Professional Course Lesson Booklet Series

# TABLET OF CONTENTS

COURSE INTRODUCTION

LESSON SIXTEEN:
ALPHA THOUGHT

APPENDIX

# PROFESSIONAL
# COURSE
# INTRODUCTION

# WELCOME, SEEKER!
## LET'S CHART YOUR JOURNEY
## ON THE PATHWAY

*Systemology* is a "holistic" approach to understanding the human experience. It is not actually a singular "subject" in itself, but rather, a new way in which to view the many subjects of *Life* and all *Existence.*

This is a professional course in *Systemology*—specifically, how to *apply* the spiritual philosophy of *Mardukite Systemology* as a personal *"Pathway" to Ascension.* Our *Systemology* is a new approach to *"Self-Actualization."* It is completely relevant for the modern age and the future; and quite different from any previous similar attempts, or other traditions, you might find. What's more: it is applicable to anyone with any background.

This *"Professional Course"* series of lessons (booklets) immediately follows the material given in the *"Basic Course"* series—available as six separate pocket-sized booklets, or in a single hardcover volume titled: *"Fundamentals of Systemology: A New Thought For The 21st Century."*

This is a *new* presentation of *Systemology*, emphasizing the application of our philosophy for those *Seekers* that are *"Flying-Solo"*—or else working through their studies and exercises as solitary practitioners. This is a new innovation for *Systemology*. Aside from the book *"Crystal Clear,"* all of our former advanced courses have placed a focus on *"Traditional Piloting"*—where experienced practitioners assist *Seekers* in *"processing."*

To receive the greatest benefit from this study: it is expected that a *Seeker* will already be familiar with the fundamental concepts and terminology (previously relayed in the *Basic Course*) before using lessons from the *Professional Course*. This will allow us to cover the extensive territory of the *Pathway* much more quickly. However, for reference, a basic *"glossary"* of vocabulary used in this lesson is provided in the *"appendix."*

---

## A NEW VIEW OF THE HUMAN SPIRIT

*Systemology* is not a religion and does not require any type of *faith*. It is, however, built upon a "spiritual" premise—and as such is an "applied spiritual philosophy." It is based on ancient teachings that we are *Spiritual Beings* essentially "wearing" bodies like clothes—or using them as "vehicles." Yet our true native nature is not *physical*, but beyond this existence; and we can certainly operate a "body" from *outside* of it.

We are **all** *Spiritual Beings*—each of us a *unit* of *Spiritual Awareness*—that have experienced a very long *Spiritual Timeline* of existence. Although we might be particularly attached to the familiar "physical shells" associated with *this* lifetime, our true *"Spiritual Lifetime"* is seemingly *eternal*. We have been many things before *Human*, and we go onward as a *Spiritual Being* after our *"genetic vehicle"* of *this* incarnation perishes.

While a "spiritual" view of the *Human Condition* may not seem unique to our philosophy, just how often is the concept treated *systematically*? For that matter: just how many people, supposedly raised to this or that religion, or professing to believe one thing or another, actually live their lives as though they are *Spirits*?

As *Spiritual Beings* of immortal existence and infinite potential, we are not simply the *"creations"* of an even greater *Being-*

*ness*; we are, in fact, an integral part of that *"creative force"* which permeates all existence.

Our basic nature is to be a *"creative being"*—our highest goals are *"to create."* And as such a being—which we refer to as an *Alpha-Spirit* in *Systemology*—we have run into some difficulties along the course of our *Spiritual Timeline* and found ourselves trapped within material *Universes* of our own collaborative *creation*.

Since we did not start out our existence in a trapped condition, it is correct to say that we have *"fallen"* from our native *"godlike"* states. It did not happen all at one, but progressively and systematically. We know our "troubles" have resulted from accumulated "barriers" and "blockages"—or *fragmentation*—during our vast experiences as *Spiritual Beings*. They are not because we lack something; but because of what's been added.

In *Systemology*, we systematically examine those routes by which we must have descended to reach our present condition, then reverse the direction of travel and chart a personal *"Pathway to Ascension."* Of course, the exact "details" of the *Spiritual Timeline* will be different for each individual *Seeker*. However, we have been able to systematically chart our *Pathway* based on common patterns of *Human fragmentation*.

In the most basic terms: the *fragmentation* that defines our "downward spiral" consists of decisions or considerations where we deny our true nature. This includes those decisions to *"withdraw"* rather than *"reach"*; where we choose to *not-know* rather than *know*; to *not-communicate* rather than *communicate*; and ultimately, to take *no-responsibility* for being a *creative-cause*, and therefore succumb to being an *effect*.

But there is *hope!* And much more importantly: there is an effectively workable *way out* of the mazes and traps of our existence. If you are reading this now, you have already begun to gather your tools and build up the *"horsepower"* necessary to break the gravity holding your *Spiritual Beingness* to the *Human Condition.*

---

## STUDYING THE PROFESSIONAL COURSE

Most *Seekers* study and practice *Systemology* at-a-distance and independent of the "Mardukite Academy" or any "Master-level" mentors trained therein. This means that the *books* (and to a lesser degree, the *internet*) are the only means of direct contact a *Seeker* maintains with the "Systemology Society" during their studies. A continuing *Seeker* from the *"Basic Course"* will be familiar with the style of study found in *this* course.

Misunderstood words are the most common reason an individual abandons studying a subject. When a misunderstanding occurs, *Awareness* declines. These misunderstandings start to "stack up" after the first occurrence, and as a result, the level of interest and attention will also decline. This is how a "confusion" develops; and the individual will get "bored" with the subject, feel tired, and unable to concentrate.

One solution is to return to the part of the material that was still interesting and enjoyable to read. When scanning around that area of text, there is likely to be a new word (or new specific use of a familiar word) that is unclear, but was passed by unnoticed. All *Systemology* books include their own *glossary*. Using this *glossary* and a high-quality dictionary will help resolve this misunderstanding once it is located.

An effective education of any subject is taught on a *gradient*. This is what is intended by presenting the study of something as "*grades*." Rather than treating a subject as one total mass, true learning is achieved by increasing one's understanding with a *gradual* increase upward. The *ascent* to a mountaintop is not successfully achieved in one leap, but by targeting and reaching specific checkpoints along the way.

This *Professional Course* consists of a series of lessons (booklets) that gradually increase a *Seeker's* ability to understand and apply the practices and techniques of *Systemology* as a complete "*Pathway to Ascension*." It is an appropriate study for continuing *Seekers* (from the *Basic Course*), but also "advanced" *Systemologists*.

Each lesson (booklet) of the *Professional Course* applies *Systemology* to a particular subject (or focus). It is best if the entire course can be studied and applied in sequential order. These lessons also employ a style of practice or technique called "*Systematic Processing.*" An introduction to applying this methodology is provided in the final lesson (booklet) of the *Basic Course*—or in the "*Fundamentals of Systemology*" volume.

To study the *Professional Course* just like a student at the Academy: a *Seeker* reads through all instructional material and applies each exercise (or "*process*") presented in the text to the extent they comfortably can, before continuing on to the next lesson (booklet).

When first starting on the *Pathway* as a *Solo* practitioner, without the aid of an experienced *Pilot*, a *Seeker* shouldn't "push too hard" or allow themselves to get too "stuck" on any one area (lesson) or *process*. It is not expected that any one area will be completely handled when first introduced. For optimum results, it is expected that a serious *Seeker* will make more than one "pass" through the entire *Professional Course.*

The *Professional Course* is not altogether different from other forms of practical or technical education: where the instruction and exercises are delivered to a completion, and then a student further increases their abilities, strength and skill-level by applying additional practice throughout their life. Therefore, a student should not concern themselves with perfectly mastering each step (or lesson) before progressing forward.

Additional passes through the material are likely to result in different "*realizations*" (an increased *level of understanding*) than a previous time. New "layers" of *Knowingness* may now be accessible during a *process* that may not have been before. It is important to avoid invalidating the progress you've made just because one area is not completely handled right away, or if a certain *process* seems too difficult on the first pass.

---

## CHARTING A COURSE ON THE PATHWAY

Although we can communicate a systematic structure to *fragmentation,* the personal journey experienced along the *Pathway* will be different for each *Seeker.* For example, certain areas will seem more *"turbulent"* or difficult for one *Seeker* than another. We tend to say that these areas have more *"charge"* on them—or that they are more *"heavily charged."* It is best to handle such areas when you are already feeling "good" and not in a situation (or condition) where that specific area is consistently being *"triggered"* or *"restimulated."*

As an applied philosophy, *Systemology* "theory" can be easily utilized in the "laboratory" of the "world-at-large" in everyday life. This is implied within the basic instruction of each lesson. Unlike other "sciences" that conduct experiments by making a change to some "objective variable" *out there* and waiting to see an effect, our focus is the individual (or *Observer*) themselves, and how *they* affect the "*Reality*" perceived.

In addition to applying *Systemology* "New Thought" to everyday life, our philosophy is applied by using specific exercises and systematic techniques. These "*processes*" provide the most stable personal gain (and *realizations*) for each area; but only when actually applied with a *Seeker's* full "*presence*" and *Awareness.*

This *Professional Course* is designed so that it may be easily read and studied with little concern for what "dangers" these teachings—or *processing*—might unleash. However, there are still some guidelines that pertain to the "best-uses" of these course lessons, particularly if a *Seeker* intends for stable development.

Skipping over too much material/*processing* in early lessons may make attempts to understand (or apply) later lessons more difficult. However, once the complete *Professional Course* is worked through at least once in its entirety, specific areas can then be later returned to and treated with a greater sense of *Awareness* and *"presence"* than before. Of course, in *"Traditional Piloting,"* the rate of processing is monitored by an experienced practitioner; but in *"Solo-Processing,"* a *Seeker* must regulate their own progress on the *Pathway*.

Applying a systematic technique is called *"running a process."* The *processes* are designed with very simple instructions or "*command-lines.*" To *run* a *processing command-line,* a *Seeker* may be assisted by the communication of that *line* from a "*Co-Pilot*" (as in "*Traditional Piloting*"). But even then, a *Seeker* must still personally "input" the *command* as *Self.* For this reason — and quite thankfully — *Solo-Processing* is possible.

---

## TAKING FLIGHT ON THE PATHWAY

*Processing Techniques* are intended to treat the *Spiritual Being* or *Alpha-Spirit*; the individual themselves. It is applied by the *Alpha-Spirit* — then *Self-directed* to the "Mind-System" or even a "body" (*genetic-vehicle*), both of which are "constructs" that the *Alpha-Spirit* (*Self,* or the "I-AM" *Awareness unit*) operates, but neither of which is actually *Self. Fragmentation* causes *Humans* to falsely identify *Self as* the "*Mind*" or even a "*Body.*"

The *Professional Course* lessons (booklets) are designed for the *Beginning Seeker* in mind—one that may have an understanding of theory, but with little experience in practice. That being said: each of these lessons may be used toward total *Beta-Defragmentation* within a specific area. There are also more *processes* given for each subject than may be necessary to achieve an *ultimate end-point realization* on that entire area.

Some *processes* can be treated quite lightly at first; others may require a bit of working at in order to get "*running*" well. It is important to set aside a period of time when you can be dedicated to your studies and *processing.* This period of time is referred to as a "*processing session.*" The reason for this, is that when a *process* does start *running* well, it is important to be able to complete it to a satisfactory "*end-point.*"

The purpose of *systematic processing* is to be able to *really* "look" at things and even determine the *considerations* we have made—or attitudes we have decided—about *Reality* as a result of those experiences. It doesn't do us much good to simply "glance"—or to *restimulate* something uncomfortable and then quickly *withdraw* from it once again, leaving more of our *attention* yet again behind and held fixedly on it.

Generally speaking, a *Seeker* continues to *run* a *process* so long as something is "happening"—which is to say, the *process* is still producing a change. Usually this is evident by the type of "answers" that a *command-line* helps a *Seeker* originate from the database of their own *Mind-System*. The *command-lines* do not "do" anything on their own. They assist a *Seeker* to direct their own attention toward increasing *Awareness*.

Of course, a *Seeker* may also cease to generate new "data" from a *process* without reaching an *"ultimate" realization* as an *"end-point."* It is possible that additional "layers" (or even other "areas") require handling before anything "deeper" is accessible. If this is the case, end the *process*. But, if a *Seeker* is *withdrawing* from something uncomfortable that was incited or stirred up, then a *process* is *run* until they feel "good" about it.

In case the thought of encountering *"turbulence"* is a concern: the techniques given as *"Opening Procedures"* of a *Formal Session* (in the *Basic Course*), and those found in the earliest lessons of the *Professional Course*, are quite useful when applied as "safety nets" for maintaining *Awareness* and *presence*, even when *Flying-Solo*.

One of the benefits to *Flying-Solo* is that *processing* is entirely *Self-determined*. This already provides a certain built-in "safety" for a practitioner. Anything you *restimulate* by *Self-determinism* is *your thing*. It is not incited by external *other-determined* influences (or other "source-points" in existence) that make you an *effect*. It can be more easily handled in *processing*—or you can simply let things "cool down" and come back to it again.

While it may seem "mysterious" to beginners, a *Seeker* gets a sense for knowing how long to *run* a *process* only with practice. Once you have spent some time actually applying the *Professional Course*, there are many aspects that become "second nature" because they are, in fact, a part of our true original nature. All we have done is *"reverse engineer"* the routes of *creation* and *consideration* that are already *our own*.

# LESSON SIXTEEN: ALPHA THOUGHT

# QUANTUM SYSTEMOLOGY

Many years ago, *archaic* or *early* presentations of our *Systemology* borrowed more *terminology* from the preexisting material sciences. The *systematic vocabulary* we use today, and for this course, continued to evolve for over a decade among those *Seekers* participating in our underground development (since *2008*).

In its early development, we noticed that the *Seekers* catching on the quickest all had something in common: a previous conceptual understanding of *"metaphysics," "physics,"* and/or *"quantum physics."* There are actually many concepts relayed in *"quantum physics"* that demonstrate an evolution in understanding by *some* scientists regarding the *"physics"* of *this Physical Universe.*

Understanding the study and unique terminology of *quantum physics* is hardly necessary for the *Pathway*. However, an *advanced Seeker* may find a "conceptual" overview quite interesting. And it is always helpful to understand the actual "*physics*" of whatever *Universe* one is "operating" from. [Such an endeavor exceeds the scope of this lesson. We direct *students* to other material for this, such as Fred Alan Wolf's "*Taking the Quantum Leap: The New Physics for Non-Scientists.*"]

One of the basic things a *Seeker* can take away from the idea of *quantum physics* is that the actual *reality* or *solidity* underlying what we observe as the *Physical Universe* is not quite as solidly fixed as conventional physics would have had us believe; that things are not all "clockwork gears" and "solid billiard balls" knocking into one another; and that an individual, themselves—"*The Observer*," as they say—actually has some participation in the *reality* of things being how they are, seem, or appear. Of course, an *advanced "Systemologist" knows* all this from their own experience, without being concerned with formulas or math.

Our *Systemology* proposes an *Infinite "background"* to *ALL Existence* that is essentially a *Nothingness*—an *Infinity-of-Nothingness*. This is, however, balanced by an *"infinite potential"* of *Somethingness*. It doesn't mean that this *infinite-everything* is experienced or manifest at once; it means that the *"potential"* for something *TO BE* is actually *limitless*. Of course, this does not rule out bringing something into *being* that will, at a certain level beneath that, *limit* the *potential*.

For example: If you hold the *decision* that you "can go anywhere" at the same time as "cannot go on a plane," you've actually *limited* your *potential* of action (or freedom); and probably are continuously creating *fragmentation* about *"planes,"* which eventually can become as *solid* as a *barrier.* Right now, we aren't concerned with where the individual goes or how—all that is relevant here is the *layers of decision* that exist.

In *quantum physics*, there is a concept called a *"probability wave"* or *"potentiality wave function."* All this means is that *all* states of *"possible existence"* are suspended in a condition of *"potential"* until they are *realized.* The analogy we might cite of *"Schrodinger's Cat"* ranks right up there with *"Pavlov's Dog"* in demonstrating just how cruel and out of touch these "scientific minds" are with the natural world they claim to understand.

As a more civil example: if you flip a "coin" so that it lands *behind* you (out of view) and there is no one yet observing the *"heads/tails"* result, then the *potential observable reality* is *simultaneously both.* The *"wave"* of *potentiality* has not yet *"collapsed"* into a *"solid reality"* of one position or another until it is actually *observed.*

At the point it is *observed*, only *one* of the possible *"positions"* or *"functions"* of the *"potentiality-wave"* becomes a *Something*; and the others fade back into *Nothingness*. This actually says a lot about our *Universe*.

While this level of participation does not *change*, for example, the molecular structure of the "coin" into something else, it demonstrates an underlying principle behind *reality*, which *"magicians"* and *"mystics"* have been attempting to *control* for a very long time—long before any *"quantum sciences"* were recognized. For the final lesson of this *Professional Course* we will approach these same areas, but *systemologically*.

## THE "COIN" EXPERIMENT

Our "coin" example from the introduction was not chosen at random. It reflects a very real experiment that a *Seeker* can play with. The basic instruction is given in the example; but note that the act of *observing* the result "*collapses the potentiality wave*" and thereafter cannot be changed. So, anything a *Seeker* might attempt to *do* or *create* (*visualize*) must take place before the "coin" is examined to see if it shows "*heads*" or "*tails*."

"*Quantum Effects*" suggest that we can influence the "*probability wave*" before it *collapses* into one position as *reality*. You "*visualize*" or "*intend*" prior to *flip-tossing* the "coin" or afterward; but any influence that might be had will end as soon as it is observed by someone. You might try *visualizing* "coin come up heads" or perhaps *create* a large *mental image* of a "coin showing heads" in front of you. If you are practiced in *ZU-Vision*: you might *look* at the "coin" while it's still behind the *Body* (with eyes closed) and *create* a *copy* of it (showing heads) hovering over the physical coin. Any specific method requires personal experimentation.

As a systematic experiment, an individual will attempt to *run* this *10 times*: performing the *visualization* and then *observing* the *reality*. Record the results in your *notebook/log* of how many times it comes up *heads* versus *tails*. You might make additional notes about the technique you used (and any other relevant data). [As an experimental procedure: conduct a *"run of 10 times"* once daily for a week and examine the results.]

Of course, mathematically, the *coin* should come up *heads* about *5 times* (*of 10*). Our data from *uninfluenced* *"runs of 10"* demonstrated that it is not uncommon for *heads* to "naturally" come up *4 to 6 times* (*of 10*). We use *"runs of 10"* because it's easy to treat as a *"percentage"* and of course we do this experiment for several days to compare results. This helps you decide if you need to alter the technique(s) being applied.

A consistent *7 times* (70%) or *greater* (of *"visualizing"* heads and having *heads* coming up) is considered a possible *probability bias* in your favor. There are other *spiritual mechanisms* that can be at play here—including a tendency to "attract negatives" (where you get *tails because* you're trying to get *heads*). For example: if consistently coming up with *3 times* or less, you may still be influencing the *probability*, but in a way where you are *unknowingly* working against yourself. [If you are applying *intention* and coming up *3 times* or less, it is likely you still have some *Beta-Defragmentation* to do.]

This experiment is simply that; an experiment. It is not, by itself, any indicator of one's own *spiritual ability*, or even a checkpoint for the *Pathway*. It's simply something fun we added that is relevant for our lesson.

## WHAT IS A "POSTULATE"?

Throughout this course (and other *Systemology* material), perhaps one of the most *esoteric* words used is: *"POSTULATE."* We tend to prefer our own term *"Alpha-Thought,"* though they really mean the same thing when treated at the highest level of *Beingness* and *Existence.* But, of course, we have merely exchanged one word for another. So, what does it actually mean? What *is* a *"postulate"*?

A specific *systematic* and *scientific* use of the word *"postulate"* began over *2000* years ago in ancient *Greece*, when the mathematician *Euclid* started systematizing an understanding of *"geometry"* for the *Greeks*. In order to do this, *Euclid's* demonstrations began with *"first principles"* that must be taken as absolute without proof. While the *Greeks* already had the word "*axiom*," it wasn't quite right for this. His "*axioms*" were *true* only when based on other even more "*basic*" statements of *truth*, which he called "*postulates*."

The word "*postulate*" comes from the *Latin* "*postulare*," meaning "*to demand*." A *postulate* stands on its own; it does not require *logic* or *reason* to *Be*; and in *Euclid's* case, truths that required no proof. From these basic truths, other *axioms* can then be established—using the *postulates* as the basis for *their logic* and *reason*. This is where we get ideas such as "a line segment connects any two points" and "parallel lines never intersect."

Where it concerns our *Systemology* of the *Alpha-Spirit*, we treat *postulates* as "*Alpha-Thought*," which is to say "*causative thought*." This is treated at "7" on our *Standard Model* and *ZU-Line*, the same position that we place the *Alpha-Spirit* on our charts. This is because at the level of *postulates* or *Alpha-Thought*, we are directly treating the *native state* of the *Alpha-Spirit* itself. When we *Imagine* or *Create* a *mental image*, we are directly "*postulating*" it *to exist* within our "*Personal Universe.*"

*Alpha-Thought* is the *origin-point* of everything that is directed from the *Alpha-Spirit* all "down" the *ZU-Line*. But our *Awareness* and *intentions* must also pass through various levels of "*implants*" and "*mental machinery*" before resulting in what we consider our *experience* of *Beta-Existence*. This is why *systematic processing* is so critical for rehabilitating *Alpha-Thought*; because our full *Self-Determinism* is being *limited* by *fragmentation*.

We have indirectly treated personal *postulates* for the entirety of the *Pathway*. It is the level of *causation* that permits an individual the *freedom* to *actually change their mind* or even *create*. The various exercises and *processes* strip away the layers of *rest-*

*riction* that remain from former *postulates* and *creations* we've forgotten.

*Postulates* are a very specific kind of "thought" that we carry around; but it is not a "thinkingness." It is a direct statement or *intention* to *Be* or *do*, or even *Not-Be* or *avoid-doing*. It may be an intention to *have* or *not-have*. The *justification-considerations* we use to make others wrong, or as reasons for our failures, are usually *postulates*. And *postulates* sometimes include absolutes like "*always*" or "*never*" — such as "I never do things right" or "I always do things wrong." The statements usually will have some *turbulent charge* on them.

Many *postulates* will include "*I*," "*I am*," or "*me*," in its wording. They are typically stated in present-time (not the future). "This is killing me" or "This kills me" is a *postulate*. "This might kill me one day" is *not*. A child trying to get out of attending school by saying "I am sick" is

44

making a *postulate*. Now, that *postulate* may not actually "*stick*" and be *reality* at that time—but, enough years of repetitively putting "*charge*" on that statement *could* result in a manifestation at any point; because *Self* does not like to be *wrong*.

In *Traditional Piloting*, a *Professional Pilot* will record the *postulates* that a *Seeker* says while *incident running* or other *systematic processes*. These are *run* after *confronting* an *incident*, &tc. This is why we instruct a *Solo-Pilot* to notice any *decisions* they made during, or as a result of, an *incident*. These *postulates* are what hold the *fragmentation* in place, and ultimately is the area we want to treat for effective and stable *defragmentation*. Most of the time, we are simply reducing the *charge* or *turbulence* in an area in order to make *confronting* things more acceptable; but *total defragmentation* also requires handling an underlying *postulate* "*As-It-Is*."

## CAUSATIVE THOUGHT

The original *native state* of an *Alpha-Spirit* includes near-infinite *creative ability*. This is what the *Alpha-Spirit* enjoyed in its highest purest form in its own *"Home Universe"* — and is mirrored in our *"Personal Universe."* At this ultimate or highest level of *spiritual ability*, the *Alpha-Spirit* is able to have "things" *exist* by simply *postulating* that they *exist* — or having things "happen" simply by *postulating* that they *are happening.*

This *"Alpha"* level of *causative thought* is what *magicians* and *New Thought practitioners* are chasing after, each in their own way. *Alpha-Thought* is not an internal activity, such as "wishing," "hoping," "praying," or "desiring" strongly for something to *Be* or *happen*. *Alpha-Thought* is an "external projection" of *thought* that "demands" manifestation in *reality*; even if that *reality* is only one's own *Universe.* Of course, there are many things we *intend* or *create* that *do* actually manifest in *Beta-Existence.* But, it is easiest to make your *postulates* work (or *"stick"*) when treating *creations knowingly* in your *Personal Universe.*

For example: *"Visualize a door."* That "door" is there; it *exists* in your *"imagination"* or *Personal Universe.* But, this is an example of a *postulate* or *Alpha-Thought.* It is not a *"request"* for the "door" to *appear* —or any application of *"effort"* in order to *create* it. *"I have a door"* or *"having a door"* is the *postulate.*

Now: *"Visualize the door opening."* Again, a *postulate*; it is *your* "door" in *your created space*; so it just *does.* Of course, even with one's own *creations*, if you were to just sit there and "look" at the "door," or even *wish* about what it should do, it wouldn't do anything. If a *Seeker* does have to start off thinking of *postulates* as similar to

47

*wishing* (for internal dialogue or something): they can "wish" to *have* the "door" open; but then *have* the "door" open. The actual *"having it open"* is the *postulate.*

Making your *postulates* work (or *"stick"*) in *the Physical Universe* is a bit more difficult. For one: it is a *Shared-Universe* that is held together by *reality-agreements* of many individuals, with each having their own *Personal Universe.* Each interacting individual is maintaining some *agreement* with *this Universe*; but they are also *postulating* things, maintaining *compulsive-continuous creations*, holding onto *counter-intentions*—albeit *unknowingly.* Most individuals on this planet are in some way affecting other individuals on this planet. And we might even say *"fragmentation is contagious."* But, highly *Actualized* individuals—able to *confront* the *games* of this existence—also have a uniquely strong ability to positively affect the world around them too.

At this stage of the *game*, an *Alpha-Spirit* is so deeply enmeshed in *reality-agreements* with *the Physical Universe* that it is rather difficult to make *Alpha-Thought* manifest directly in *Beta-Existence*. By *Alpha-Thought* we mean *intentions* that *materialize* while bypassing Physical Laws; or in other words "*magic*."

One's own *considerations* and *counter-intentions*, not to mention out-of-sight *spiritual machinery*, all contribute to "*dampening*" or "*limiting*" direct material manifestations of our *spiritual ability*. And by this, we do *not* necessarily mean literal demonstrations of "pulling rabbits from thin air" or "making solid forms disappear." But we *do* mean the kinds of things that individuals are likely to "*wish*" about, or even "*cast spells*" for, *&tc.*

Unlike other approaches to "personal development," our *Systemology* emphasizes *defragmentation* rather than starting off with attempts to manifest *causative thought*—such as you find with typical *New Age* and *New Thought* traditions. Much like the handling of *"energy"* and *"energy beams"* (in former lessons), there is a lot of potential *invalidation* to overcome when applying techniques directly to *the Physical Universe*. When this happens too much, it tends to reinforce a conviction that *"Beta-Existence* is *right*; and we are *wrong."*

The easiest *postulates* to make "stick" are those you make for the benefit of others rather than yourself. You could still directly benefit from this, if you are able to *postulate* things for others in a way that also brings you what you need as a byproduct. But really, don't get too frustrated if you don't get immediate results.

Our entire *Systemology* is in many ways a study (and handling) of the *considerations* and *counter-intentions* that block our *Alpha-Thought* (or *spiritual ability*) from being as high-powered as we can be in our *native state.* Your *native state* is not "lost" to you—because it *is you*; simply "hidden" by *fragmentation.* And in *our tradition,* this progressive uncovering and clearing of *Self* is what we treat as the *Pathway to Ascension.*

## HANDLING "POSTULATES"

During our time in *the Physical Universe,* many of our *postulates* are automatically "stopped" by a simultaneously made *counter-postulate.* There are *reality-agreements* and *spiritual machinery* that contributes to this. But, this is what can actually keep our *energies* in "suspension" as a *wave-ridge* or *restriction* in the *flow.* In essence, it becomes like two of our *flows* colliding together, creating a *wave-peak* (like two land masses pushing together to make a mountain ridge).

What we are describing is really the *ener-*

*getic-mass* that entangles our *Awareness* in *fragmentation* progressively throughout our *spiritual history*. It puts more of our *postulates*, our *Alpha-Thought*, our *spiritual power*, in a suspended state of *uncertainty*; our decisions to *"Be"* or *"Not-Be"* turn into *"maybe."* In other cases: we *"must have"* but *"can't have"* and now we *"don't have"* and then some of our *attention* remains perpetually fixed thereafter in a state of *confusion*.

• Let's *knowingly* practice a simple exercise that illustrates just some of what is taking place *unknowingly*. For this you will need a small object such as a *pencil*. We want to use a simple *postulate*, such as: *"reaching over and moving the pencil."*

–First: you will actually do it a few times; make the *postulate*, then move the *pencil*. Now: *postulate* "moving" it; then immediately change your mind, and *postulate* "not moving" it (and leave the *pencil* where it is).

52

—Next, we want to focus on mentally "re-laxing" two *postulates* that are being "held" (or *maintained, created, &tc.*) in op-position to each other. Now: *postulate* both *intentions* simultaneously ("moving" and "not moving" the *pencil*) and "hold" them for a moment; then "relax."

As you hold the two *postulates* simultan-eously: you may notice, or get the sense of, a *tension, mass,* or *solidity* forming that seems to dissipate or fall away when you relax. Part of this practice is learning how to *relax* the hold—or *release* the "charge"—on *postulates* that are held in suspension like this.

\*\*\* In *systematic processing*: *postulates* are typically handled like "*command-items*" of an *Implant* (see *Lesson-11*); and for good reason—"*command-items*" are basically *implanted postulates*. One of the reasons we use alternating *processing com-mand-lines* in our *defragmentation* is to take *charge* off unseen *considerations* and *counter-intentions* too.

If there is still a doubt in the *Seeker's* thoughts as to their participation in the experience of *solidity* in *this Physical Universe*: *running* the following *postulates* as a *process* (each by themselves, alternating, then simultaneously and relaxing) probably won't make the world go away; but at least you'll have a better idea of what you're dealing with, and why you sometimes get a strong feeling that things aren't real when they are. [And if there was some obscure concise *"upper-level secret"* for this course, here in our final lesson, than this is it.]

> The most basic *postulate-counter-postulate* we all carry with us (*compulsively create*) that provides *Beta-Existence* its continuing *wave-ridge solidity* is:
>
> ~*There is nothing there.*
> ~*There is something there.*

## POSITIVE "AFFIRMATIONS"

Perhaps the most appropriate parallel to *Alpha-Thought* that we find in the contemporary *New Age* and *New Thought* movements, is the emphasis on *"affirmations,"* *"intention,"* and *"attraction."* These areas are not always handled or communicated properly; but this provides at least a basis for what we are talking about.

Repetitive *"positive affirmations"* are a way of applying *intention* over and over again, like hammering a nail, with a gentle *demand* that it become *reality.* This is very much like making a *postulate*; but in this case, a proper systematic handling of *"affirmations"* and *"positive intention"* is the most communicable and accessible way to treat the subject of *Alpha-Thought* as we bring this *Professional Course* to a close.

Any kind of *"charged"* consideration can

affect your own view of yourself, or how you experience your own *reality* (or *Personal Universe*); and naturally, this alone can contribute to how you carry yourself in the *Game of Life*—what you do, how you act, *&tc*. This is what underlies all *"motivational coaching"* and similar things. But when most *Seekers* think of *Alpha-Thought*, it concerns a *spiritual ability* to directly influence *reality* itself.

Just as we have our own *spiritual machinery* (described in *Lesson-14*), there is larger-scale *spiritual machinery* for *manifesting reality*. If our personal *Implant-Platforms* are any indicator, this *reality-machinery* is likely operating on many *lines of programmed-code* (like *"command-items"* of an *Implant*) as an *"operating-system."* A lot of *mystics* have called it a *"universal mind"* or *"cosmic consciousness."* It may even be a fragmented part of ourselves that we threw into the "pool" when this *Beta-Existence* was constructed.

Most importantly: this *reality-machine* seems to arbitrarily project whatever is *imprinted* on it (or *repeated*) the most: taking what *persists* on the path that least *resists* toward manifestation. The idea behind *"positive affirmation"* is that if you repeat the *thought* enough and keep uploading into this *cosmic mind*, then you eventually shift the odds of the *reality probability-wave* a bit more in your favor. This is as much as can be reasonably expected given how many individuals in this *Shared-Universe* are also projecting *thoughts* and *intentions* into this *machinery*.

When handling any kind of *Alpha-Thought*, an individual has to be careful of their *exact wording*. Mistakes discovered early on with this likely led to an almost instinctual superstition surrounding *mispronouncing* or *misstating* any *"magic words."* Because the only time this is a real concern is when we compose the *intention* or apply *Alpha-Thought*; it certainly has nothing to do with some inability to pronounce foreign languages.

Just like a *postulate*, an effective *positive affirmation* — or *"Alphamation"* — must be stated as happening in present-time, not in the *future*. Saying *"I will be..."* is a *postulate* made for a *future* that will never manifest as the *present*. The *postulate* will go on perpetually as *"for the future."* *Reality* only consist of *"Now"* at any given moment — and so this very literal *reality-machine* really has no conception of anything related to "time." There is, however, usually some delay before anything manifests as *reality*.

*Alpha-Thought* is most effective when applied in favor of yourself or someone else; and never against someone. If you are in a *competition* or *game-condition*, you *affirm* or *postulate* in favor of yourself and your own ability; not that another's will be lesser, *&tc*. There are a lot of *"protections"* and "*defense mechanisms*" built into your own *Mind-System* and that of others, so it's best to improve yourself and not get involved with using *Alpha-Thought* for revenge or harm. That's one reason we ended up *down here* in the first place.

In most cases, *positive affirmations* and *Alpha-Thought* for one's own favor do not generally stir up trouble—except in cases of *fragmentation* in a the area you are treating. In extreme cases, a *positive affirmation* can trigger *fragmentation* attached to the "*negative*" side, and the *opposite* of what's *intended* will manifest. This is when even the most well-intended *New Ager* can still find themselves facing a "*psychic backlash*" from their efforts. If a *Seeker* finds this happening at all, they need to *spot* and *confront* the source of *fragmentation* before adding more *intention* (or *charge*) to that area. Use the appropriate *processing* as learned on the course.

When *"positive affirmations"* are made about one's *Self*, the energy cycles through our own *personal energy-system* and whatever *spiritual machinery* we maintain. It can *restimulate turbulence* from *unknown* and *unconfronted* areas and manifest "negative" results. A *"backlash"* is not just a "null" result where nothing happens; at the very least, it produces undesirable personal *"emotional states."*

For example: the *affirmation* "I am rich" might restimulate *charged considerations* that "only criminals are rich" or "rich people are all corrupt," *&tc.* that originate from this lifetime or earlier ones. And it is likely part of a *"chain of incidents"* not yet *confronted*, which leads to lingering *considerations* that are *unknowingly* maintained as ones' own *beliefs* or *postulates*. Perhaps you "embezzled from a company" in a former life, and "protested about wages" in another, then became a "loan shark" in one; this could all establish heavy *fragmentation* around the basic *postulate* of *"being rich."*

One way around our own *spiritual machinery* is to start off by making the *positive affirmation* for others; *intending* them to receive, or be endowed with, the characteristic or thing we want to manifest. This can be done with a specific person, or you can go to a public place and just make the *affirmation* a few times for each person you see. Since they are external to you, there is less chance of triggering your own *machinery;* and since it is a *positive affirmation* for another, it is not likely to trigger any of their *defense-mechanisms.*

There is another reason why you might want to start off with projecting a *"repetitive affirmation"* to an external target. Much like using a *"repetitive command-line"* in *systematic processing,* this focus of *attention* has an ability to bring other *associated data* and *considerations* up to the "surface" for inspection/analysis.

This means *postulating others "being rich"* may *resurface* the *fragmented considerations* (such as "all rich people are criminals") that need to be *confronted "As-It-Is"* in order to no longer remain a personal "*barrier.*"

Additionally, we can also approach our *goals* from different directions. For example: if *"being rich"* is not working well as a *postulate/affirmation* directly, then perhaps *"being a more valuable employee"* (or something similar) might *"stick"*—and you still reach the same ends. However, it requires some work on your part still. Although *affirmations* may boost *confidence* and radiate an "*aura*" of *success* (that others can pick up on), it does not substitute having the skills or learning that may be necessary for applying it to *this Game*. So, an individual requires *Self-Honesty* and a *systematic* approach in order to effectively shape *reality*.

## HANDLING THE "NEGATIVES"

We carry a lot of internal *"protections"* or *"buffers"* that prevent "idle" and "free-wheeling" *thoughts* from instantly and spontaneously manifesting within *Beta-Existence*. A single *thought* is generally not charged or powerful enough to be harmful or destructive. We are permitted to *consider* things or *create mental imagery* in order to look at, or contemplate, without repercussions. Of course, if it *restimulates* some *fragmentation*, then that requires handling anyways. But it is a bad practice to go around putting a lot of effort into *avoiding* (or *withdrawing* from) a certain *thought* (or area) in fear that it will manifest negatively in *reality*.

While a single *thought* is not particularly destructive: *repetition* and *emotional charge* can certainly be. What we mean here is any *negative postulates* that an individual likely *repeats* throughout everyday life—whether to themselves or in communication with others. For example: "I'm stupid" or "I'm always so clumsy"—these types of *postulates*, if *repeated* enough with conviction (and not as repetitive technique for *knowingly processing-out "charge"*), have a tendency to manifest (or "*stick*") more easily in our experience of life.

Our *systematic processing* methods do treat a lot of "negative" expressions in our lives; generally, *fragmented* content is not particularly "fun" to handle. But when we *knowingly* treat things in *processing*, we also *systematically* balance it with the "positives." But both sides must be handled. This is because it is quite difficult to "push" the "positive" side of an area into reality when so much of the "negative" side has been reinforced and validated. Without treating the *charge* on an earlier *postulate* of "*being stupid*," no gains can be expected from a single moment of now desiring to *"be smart."* Only when you can take all of the *charge* or *fragmentation* off of both sides of a former *consideration* will a *Seeker* be completely free to *postulate* anew.

We apply *"conceptual processing"* in *Traditional Piloting* to "loosen up" a certain area by *getting a sense* of the "concept" of actually "being" two different opposing conditions. For example: alternating *"get a sense of being rich"* and *"get a sense of being poor."* Alternating them this way in *processing* does not actually manifest these states or even add any *charge* to them. There is another reason we do this as well. In order to *postulate* a state of *"being rich,"* the *Alpha-Spirit* must necessarily *postulate* that a state of *"being poor"* also *exists*. This is the part that tends to get overlooked in *New Age* or *New Thought* materials; and the only remedy that we have found for effectively handling the "total package" of the *Human Condition* is the regimen of *systematic processing* described throughout the lessons of this course.

## THE RITE OF ALPHA-THOUGHT

As we bring both this lesson and the entire *Professional Course* to a close, it seems like there should be "something" presented here at the end—that it has all been leading up to something "definitive" or "finite." Of course, the personal gains, *realizations*, and rehabilitation of *ability* takes place all throughout the course. And as has been suggested, a *Seeker* reaches a new level on their second pass through the course, starting from the beginning. It is not the *same* course when you do it again. Suddenly things start "clicking" better that seemed difficult before; or new deeper layers of *fragmentation* will *resurface*.

At the same time, we *are* reaching a completion-point of the actual instructional material given for this course. In other more *esoteric* traditions, a *Seeker* might receive an "initiation" ceremony, or get "installed" to a higher "grade" or "office" within the organization. Or, as a sign of "achievement," those traditions of a more *mystical* style might entrust a special *"spell-scroll"* or *"secret ritual"* that would somehow demonstrate a practical summation of all they had learned. This last one sounds like more *fun* for our purposes.

As a final technique, the present author has decided to incorporate a unique blend of *mystical* and *New Thought* methods to propose a "ritual" of sorts to aid a *Seeker* in more easily accessing *Alpha-Thought* and applying it to achieving their *goals*. It may be that applying what techniques still remain effective from our time in the *Magic Universe*, in order to play the *game* in *this Universe*, is the *only* way to even approach a "win" without mistakenly applying *force* against *force*, or becoming more ingrained in *reality-agreements* of *this world*. That is a matter we leave for a *Seeker* to determine as they achieve *higher levels* of *Knowing*.

By *"ritual"* or *"rite"* we mean a predetermined systematized arrangement of steps —not altogether different from the structure of a *"Formal Session."* There is no real *"occult"* tone intended otherwise. The only spirit summoned by this is the *Alpha-Spirit*, the highest level of *presence* of one's own *Self*, preferably as an *Actualized Awareness* that is free from heavy *fragmentation*.

This technique is no more "supernatural" than any of the others that we have discussed in prior lessons. However, it reflects a very ancient formula that has been held in veneration for its effectiveness. It is also not an inherent part of the

*Pathway*, or any kind of *defragmentation* procedure. It is something one *does* as a part of participating in the *game* apart from being *in-session*. To the "uninitiated" that has not worked along the *Pathway* to this point, it may appear indistinguishable from other popular *visualization* techniques. It's power comes from the individual—from direct *Alpha-Thought*—and not by performing complicated actions or memorizing bad poetry to recite. Unsurprisingly, we will formalize this *rite* as *seven steps*.

STEP 1: *Clearly Define the Target and Postulate.*

Avoid "specific targets" (a *certain person* or a *particular company*). Use "general targets" (a "*girlfriend*" or a "*well paying job*"). Avoid referencing "time" in *postulates* —"having a job"; *not* "getting a job"—so that the *intention* and later *visualization* is of "*Now.*" Avoid any "negative" *intentions* (such as against others).

69

STEP 2: *Defragment the Negative Side.*

Start with *conceptually running* alternate opposing statements. As good practice for more advanced work: a *systematic processing command-line* should negate the target or *terminal* and not the *condition*. For example: use "*I have a girlfriend / I have no girlfriend*" rather than "*I have a girlfriend / I don't have a girlfriend*," because to be *systematically* correct, the "negative side" is also a *condition* of "*havingness*." It is also the "side" that an individual might still be strongly *postulating* for themselves. Any *turbulence* or *fragmentation* should be at least quieted down before proceeding. Use material from the course lessons to get the area under *control*.

STEP 3: *Generate Enthusiasm.*

In other traditions, this might be stated as "*raising personal energy.*" We worked with *emotional states* and *Beta-Awareness* very early on this course. Naturally, we don't want to develop an obsessive desire or compulsion—but we have to *actually want* the *postulate* to come about if using a "positive" technique. When we expect, believe, or know something is happening, we tend to be more genuinely excited about it.

STEP 4: *See That Source Can Do It.*

*Realizing* that something is possible is the first step to making it *actual.* We are, each of us, *fragments* of an *Infinite Source*, balancing the *Nothingness* with the experience of an existence that contains potential *Everythingness.* If it helps a *Seeker* to *consider* that "*God*" can do it (as an expression of *Infinity*); or that the "*Cosmic Mind*" (*Reality-Machinery*) can produce it, just go with what's comfortable. Whatever it is you *conceive* as *manifesting reality,* know that what you are *postulating* is within their capabilities to manifest.

STEP 5: *See That You Are Source.*

*Postulates* are *causative thought*; and they only *"stick"* when projected strongly from a *Cause* or *"source-point."* Whatever it is you *conceive* as *"Source"* — and even *"God"* for this *Universe,* or *"Reality-Making Machinery"* — know that *you* are a part of *IT*, an integral interactive part of whatever *"IT"* is. There are a lot of other individuals that are a part of it too. But the *"drops"* you add to this *"pool"* have the ability to permeate the entire *"ocean."* Your *postulates* have an ability to ripple across the *Spheres of Existence* into real manifestation.

STEP 6: *See It As Happening.*

Now, *you,* as *Source,* then *"see"* that the thing or target-item is *"done"* or *"complete"* — *visualizing* or *creating mental imagery* of it *happening now* (not at some future point). Consider the example with the "door" earlier in this lesson: we aren't *postulating* that it will eventually happen; but that it is happening (or has happened right in front of us). In *Beta-Existence*, you *postulate/demand* it *exist* within that "*reality-wave*" that is constantly being generated. It might take some time, given the manifestation delays of *this reality*, but the *intention* is made and complete.

STEP 7: *Acknowledgment.*

The final step of this ritual is the completion of a cycle: we express *gratitude* and *acknowledgment* as though it has been materially presented to us and received. Recall the last time you received something you were expecting or wanting very much. That is the concept we want to project before ending our ritual. Whether we see it as being directed to "*God*" or a "*group mind*" of some sort, we *acknowledge* that it has happened; that we are *grateful* for our manifestations brightening not only our own lives, but also enriching the *Game* that we all share. Then take the culmination of your whole ritual —almost as though it were an *implanting-incident*—and strongly *project* or "upload" it into the *Universal Reality* as a single *postulate*, and completely "release it" (or "let go") knowing it is done.

This lesson marks the completion of
*The Systemology Professional Course.*
You are invited back next year for:
*The Systemology Advanced Training Course.*

# GLOSSARY

**actualization** : to make actual, not just potential; to bring into full solid Reality; to realize fully in *Awareness* as a "thing."

**agreement (reality)** : unanimity of opinion of what is "thought" to be known; an accepted arrangement of how things are; things we consider as "real" or as an "is" of "reality"; a consensus of what is real as made by standard-issue (common) participants; what an individual contributes to or accepts as "real"; in *Systemology*, a synonym for "*reality*."

**alpha** : the first, primary, basic, superior or beginning of some form; in *Systemology*, referring to the state of existence operating on spiritual archetypes and postulates, will and intention "exterior" to the low-level condensation and solidarity of energy and matter as the 'physical universe' (*beta*).

**alpha-spirit** : a "spiritual" *Life*-form; the "true" *Self* or I-AM; the *individual*; the spiritual (*alpha*) *Self* that is animating the (*beta*) physical body or "*genetic vehicle*" using a continuous *Lifeline* of spiritual ("*ZU*") energy; an individual spiritual (*alpha*) entity possessing no physical mass or measurable waveform (motion) in the Physical Universe as itself, so it animates the (*beta*) physical body or "*genetic vehicle*" as a catalyst to experience *Self*-determined causality in effect within the *Physical Universe*; a singular unit or point of *Spiritual Awareness* that is *Aware* that it is *Aware.*

**alpha thought** : the highest spiritual *Self-determination* over creation and existence exercised by an Alpha-Spirit; the Alpha range of pure *Creative Ability* based on direct postulates and considerations of *Beingness*; spiritual qualities comparable to "thought" but originating in Alpha-existence, independently superior to a Mind-System.

**ascension** : actualized *Awareness* elevated to the point of true "spiritual existence" exterior to *beta existence*. An "Ascended Master" is one who has returned to an incarnation on Earth as an inherently *Enlightened One*, demonstrable in their words and actions; they have the ability to *Self-direct* the "Mind" and "Body" as *Self* (as a "Spirit"); and to maintain consciousness as a personal identity continuum with the same *Self-directed* control and communication of Will-Intention that is exercised, actualized and developed deliberately during one's present incarnation.

**associative knowledge** : significance or meaning of a facet or aspect assigned to (or considered to have) a direct relationship with another facet; to connect or relate ideas or facets of existence with one another; in traditional systems logic, an equivalency of significance or meaning between facets or sets that are grouped together, such as in *(a + b) + c = a + (b + c)*; in Systemology, erroneous associative knowledge is assignment of the same value to all facets or parts considered as related (even when they are not actually so), such as in *a = a, b = a, c = a* and so forth without distinction.

**attention** : active use of *Awareness* toward a specific aspect or thing; the act of "attending" with the presence of *Self*; a direction of focus or concentration of *Awareness* along a particular channel or conduit or toward a particular terminal node or communication termination point; the Self-directed concentration of personal energy as a combination of observation, thought-waves and consideration; focused application of *Self-Directed Awareness*.

**awareness** : the highest sense of-and-as *Self* in knowing and being as I-AM (the *Alpha-Spirit*); the extent of beingness directed as a viewpoint (POV) experienced by *Self* as *Knowingness*.

**beta (awareness)** : all consciousness activity ("*Awareness*") in the "Physical Universe" (KI, in *Zuism*) or else in *beta-existence*; *Awareness* within the range of the *genetic-body*, including material thoughts, emotional responses and physical motors; personal *Awareness* of physical energy and physical matter moving through physical space and experienced as "time"; the *Awareness* held by *Self* that is restricted to an organic *Lifeform* or "*genetic vehicle*" in which it experiences causality in *beta-existence*.

**beta (existence)** : all manifestation in the "Physical Universe" (KI, in *Zuism*); the conditions of *Awareness* for the *Alpha-spirit* (*Self*) as a physical organic *Lifeform* or "*genetic vehicle*" in which it experiences causality in the *Physical Universe*.

**charge** : to fill or furnish with a quality; to supply with energy; to lay a command upon; in *Systemology*—to imbue with intention; to overspread with emotion; personal energy stores and significances entwined as fragmentation in mental images, reactive-response encoding and intellectual (and/or) programmed beliefs.

**channel** : a specific stream, course, current, direction or route; to form or cut a groove or ridge or otherwise guide along a specific course; a direct path; an artificial aqueduct created to connect two water bodies or water or make travel possible.

**circuit** : a circular path or loop; a closed-path within a system that allows a flow; a pattern or action or wave movement that follows a specific route or potential path only; in *Systemology*, "*communication processing*" pertaining to a specific *flow* of energy or information along a channel; "*feedback loop.*"

**communication** : successful transmission of information, data, energy (&tc.) along a message line, with a reception of feedback; an energetic flow of intention to cause an effect (or duplication) at a distance; the personal energy moved or acted upon by will or else 'selective directed attention'; the 'messenger action' used to transmit and receive energy across a medium; also relay of energy, a message or signal—or even locating a personal POV (viewpoint) for the Self—along the *ZU-line*.

**condense (condensation)** : the transition of vapor to liquid; denoting a change in state to a more substantial or solid condition; leading to a more compact or solid form.

**confront** : to come around in front of; to be in the presence of; to stand in front of, or in the face of; to meet "face-to-face" or "face-up-to"; additionally, in *Systemology*, to fully tolerate or acceptably withstand an encounter with a particular manifestation without an automatic reactive response.

**consideration** : careful analytical reflection of all aspects; deliberation; determining the significance of a "thing" in relation to similarity or dissimilarity to other "things"; evaluation of facts and importance of certain facts; thorough examination of all aspects related to, or important for, making a decision; the analysis of consequences and estimation of significance when making decisions; also in *Systemology*, the *postulate* or *Alpha-Thought* that defines the state of *beingness* for what something "*is.*"

**defragmentation** : the *reparation* of wholeness; collecting all dispersed parts to reform an original whole; a process of removing "*fragmentation*" in data or knowledge to provide a clear understanding; applying techniques and processes that promote a *holistic* interconnected *alpha* state, favoring observational *Awareness* of continuity in all spiritual and physical systems; in *Systemology*, a "*Seeker*" achieving actualized "*Self-Honest Awareness*" is said to be in a basic state of *beta-defragmentation*, whereas *Alpha-defragmentation* is the rehabilitation of the *creative ability*, managing the *Spiritual Timeline* and the POV of *Self* as Alpha-Spirit (I-AM).

**existence** : the *state* or fact of *apparent manifestation*; the resulting combination of the Principles of Manifestation: consciousness, motion and substance; continued *survival*; that which independently exists.

**exterior** : outside of; on the outside; in *System-ology*, we mean specifically the POV of *Self* that is *'outside of'* the *Human Condition,* free of the physical and mental trappings of the Physical Universe; a metahuman range of consideration; see also *'Zu-Vision'*.

**external** : a force coming from outside; inform-ation received from outside sources; in *System-ology*, the objective *'Physical Universe'* exist-ence, or *beta-existence*, that the Physical Body or *genetic vehicle* is essentially *anchored* to for its considerations of locational space-time as a dimension or POV.

**fragmentation** : breaking into parts and scatter-ing the pieces; the *fractioning* of wholeness or the *fracture* of a holistic interconnected *alpha* state, favoring observational *Awareness* of per-ceived connectivity between parts; *discontinu-ity*; separation of a totality into parts; in *Systemology*, a person outside of *Self-Honesty* is said to be operating from a *fragmented* state.

**flow** : movement across (or through) a channel (or conduit); a direction of active energetic mo-tion, typically distinguished as either an *in-flow*, *out-flow* or *cross-flow*.

**genetic-vehicle** : a physical *Life*-form; the physical (*beta*) body that is animated/controlled by the (*Alpha*) *Spirit* using a continuous *Spiritual Lifeline* (ZU); a physical (*beta*) organic receptacle and catalyst for the (*Alpha*) *Self* to operate "causes" and experience "effects" within the *Physical Universe*.

**harmful-act** : a counter-survival mode of behavior or action (esp. that causes harm to one of more *Spheres of Existence*)—or—an overtly aggressive (hostile and/or destructive) action against an individual or any other *Sphere of Existence*; in *Utilitarian Systemology*—a shortsighted (serves fewest/lowest *Spheres of Existence*) intentional overtly harmful action to resolve a perceived problem; a revision of the rule for standard *Utilitarianism* for Systemology to distinguish actions which provide the least benefit to the least number of *Spheres of Existence*, or else the greatest harm to the greatest number of *Spheres of Existence*; in *moral philosophy*—an action which can be experienced by few and/or which one would not be willing to experience for themselves (*theft, slander, rape, &tc*); an iniquity or iniquitous act.

**hold-back** : withheld communications (esp. actions) such as "*Hold-Outs*"; intentional (or automatic) withdrawal (as opposed to reach); Self-restraint (which may eventually be enforced or automated); not reaching, acting or expressing, when one should be; an ability that is now restrained (on automatic) due to inability to withhold it on Self-determinism alone.

**hold-outs** : in photography, the numerous snapshots/pictures withheld from the final display or professional presentation of the event; withheld communications; in Utilitarian Systemology— energetic withdrawal and communication breaks with a "*terminal*" and its *Sphere of Existence* as a result of a "*Harmful-Act*"; unspoken or undiscovered (hidden, covert) actions that an individual withholds communications of, fearing punishment or endangerment of *Self-preservation* (*First Sphere*); the act of hiding (or keeping hidden) the truth of a "*Harmful-Act*"; a refusal to communicate with a *Pilot*; also "*Hold-Back.*"

**holistic** : the examination of interconnected systems as encompassing something greater than the *sum* of their "parts."

**Human Condition** : a standard default state of Human experience that is generally accepted to be the extent of its potential identity (*beingness*) —currently treated as *Homo Sapiens Sapiens,* but which is scheduled for replacement by *Homo Novus* (the "New Human").

**imagination** : ability to create *mental imagery* in one's Personal Universe at will and change or alter it as desired; the ability to create, change and dissolve mental images on command or as an act of will; to create a mental image or have associated imagery displayed (or "conjured") in the mind that may or may not be treated as real (or memory recall) and may or may not accurately duplicate objective reality; to employ *creative abilities* of the Spirit that are independent of reality agreements with beta-existence.

**imprint** : to strongly impress, stamp, mark (or outline) onto a softer 'impressible' substance; to mark with pressure onto a surface; in *Systemology*, used to indicate permanent Reality impressions marked by frequencies, energies or interactions experienced during periods of emotional distress, pain, unconsciousness, loss, enforcement, or something antagonistic to physical (personal) survival, all of which are are stored with other reactive response-mechanisms at lower-levels of *Awareness* as opposed to the active memory database and proactive processing center of the Mind; an experiential "memory-set" that may later resurface—be triggered or stimulated artificially—as Reality, of which similar responses will be engaged automatically; holographic-like imagery "stamped" onto consciousness as composed of energetic *facets* tied to the "snap-shot" of an experience.

**imprinting incident** : the first or original event

instance communicated and *emotionally encoded* onto an individual's "*Spiritual Timeline*" (recorded memory from all lifetimes), which formed a permanent impression that is later used to mechanistically treat future contact on that channel; the first or original occurrence of some particular *facet* or mental image related to a certain type of *encoded response*, such as pain and discomfort, losses and victimization, and even the acts that we have taken against others along the *Spiritual Timeline* of our existence that caused them to also be *Imprinted*.

**intention** : directed application of Will; to intend (have "in Mind") or signify (give "significance" to) for or toward a particular purpose; in *Systemology* (from the *Standard Model*)—the spiritual activity at WILL (5.0) directed by an *Alpha Spirit* (7.0); the application of WILL as "Cause" from a higher order of Alpha Thought and consideration (6.0).

**interior** : inside of; on the inside; in *Systemology*, we mean specifically the POV of *Self* that is fixed to the *'internal' Human Condition,* including the *Reactive Control Center* (RCC) and Mind-System or *Master Control Center* (MCC); within *beta-existence*.

**internal** : a force coming from inside; information received from inside sources; in *Systemology*, the objective experience of *beta-existence* associated with the Physical Body or *genetic vehicle* and its POV regarding sensation and perception; from inside the body; in the body.

**invalidate** : decrease the level or degree or *agreement* as Reality.

**mental image** : a subjectively experienced "picture" created and imagined into being by the Alpha-Spirit (or at lower levels, one of its automated mechanisms) that includes all perceptible *facets* of totally immersive scene, which may be forms originated by an individual, or a "facsimile-copy" ("snap-shot") of something seen or encountered; a duplication of wave-forms in one's Personal Universe as a "picture" that mirror an "external" Universe experience, such as an *Imprint*.

**perception** : internalized processing of data received by the *senses*; to become *Aware of* via the senses.

**pilot** : a professional steersman responsible for healthy functional operation of a ship toward a specific destination; in *Systemology*, an intensive trained individual qualified to specially apply *Systemology Processing* to assist other *Seekers* on the *Pathway*.

**point-of-view (POV)** : a point to view from; an opinion or attitude as expressed from a specific identity-phase; a specific standpoint or vantage-point; a definitive manner of consideration specific to an individual phase or identity; a place or position affording a specific view or vantage; circumstances and programming of an individual that is conducive to a particular response, consideration or belief-set (paradigm); a position (consideration) or place (location) that provides a specific view or perspective (subjective) on experience (of the objective).

**postulate** : to put forward as truth; to suggest or assume an existence *to be*; to state or affirm the existence of particular conditions; to provide a basis of reasoning and belief; a basic theory accepted as fact; in *Systemology*, Alpha-Thought —the top-most decisions or considerations made by the Alpha-Spirit regarding the "*isness*" (what things "are") about energy-matter and space-time.

**presence** : a quality of some thing (*energy/matter*) being "present" in space-time; personal orientation of *Self* as an *Awareness* (*POV*) located in present space-time (environment) and communicating with extant energy-matter.

**processing command line (PCL)** : a directed input; a specific command using highly selective language for *Systemology Processing*; a predetermined directive statement (cause) intended to focus concentrated attention (effect).

**processing, systematic** : the inner-workings or "through-put" result of systems; in *Systemology*, a method of applied spiritual technology used toward personal Self-Actualization; methods of selective directed attention, communicated language and associative imagery that increases personal control of the human condition.

**realization** : the clear perception of an understanding; a consideration or understanding on what is "actual"; to make "real" or give "reality" to so as to grant a property of "being-ness" or "being as it is"; the state or instance of coming to an *Awareness*; in *Systemology*, "gnosis" or true knowledge achieved during *systematic processing*; achievement of a new (or higher) cognition, true knowledge or perception of Self; a consideration of reality or assignment of meaning.

**responsibility** : the *ability* to *respond*; the extent of mobilizing *power* and *understanding* an individual maintains as *Awareness* to enact *change*; the proactive ability to *Self-direct* and make decisions independent of an outside authority.

**Seeker** : an individual on the *Pathway to Self-Honesty*; a practitioner of *Mardukite Systemology* or *Systemology Processing*, that is working toward *Spiritual Ascension*.

**Self-actualization** : bringing the full potential of the Human spirit into Reality; expressing full capabilities and creativeness of the *Alpha-Spirit*.

**Self-determinism** : the freedom to act, clear of external control or influence; the personal control of Will to direct intention.

**Self-honesty** : the basic or original *alpha* state of *being* and *knowing*; clear and present total *Awareness* of-and-as *Self*, in its most basic and true proactive expression of itself as *Spirit* or *I-AM*—free of artificial attachments, perceptive filters and other emotionally-reactive or mentally-conditioned programming imposed on the human condition by the systematized physical world; the ability to experience existence without judgment.

**spiritual timeline** : a continuous stream of moment-to-moment *Mental Images* (or a record of experiences) that defines the "past" of a spiritual being (or *Alpha-Spirit*) and which includes impressions (*imprints, &tc.*) from all life-incarnations and significant spiritual events the being has encountered; in Systemology, also "*backtrack.*"

**Spheres of Existence** : a series of *eight* concentric circles, rings or spheres (each larger than the former) that is overlaid onto the Standard Model of Beta-Existence to demonstrate the dynamic systems of existence extending out from the POV of Self (often as a "body") at the *First Sphere*; these are given in the basic eightfold systems as: *Self*, *Home/Family*, *Groups*, *Humanity*, *Life on Earth*, *Physical Universe*, *Spiritual Universe* and *Infinity-Divinity*.

**Systemology** : a modern tradition of applied religious philosophy and spiritual technology based on *Arcane Tablets* (in combination with "*general systemology*" and "*games theory*") developed in the New Age underground by Joshua Free in 2011 as an advanced futurist extension of the *Mardukite Research Org.*

**terminal (node)** : a point, end, or mass, on a line; a connection point for closing an electric circuit, such as a post on a battery terminating at each end of its own systematic function; a point of connectivity with other points; in systems, a contact point of interaction; a point of interaction with other points.

**turbulence** : a quality or state of distortion or disturbance that creates irregularity of a flow or pattern; the quality or state of aberration on a line (such as ragged edges) or the emotional "turbulent feelings" attached to a particular flow or terminal node; a violent, haphazard or disharmonious commotion (such as in the ebb of gusts and lulls of wind action).

**validation** : a reinforcement of agreements or considerations as being "real."

**viewpoint** : see *"point-of-view" (POV).*

**willingness** : the state of conscious Self-determined ability and interest (directed attention) to *Be*, *Do* or *Have*; a Self-determined consideration to reach, face up to (*confront*) or manage some "mass" or energy; the extent to which an individual considers themselves able to participate, act or communicate along some line, to put attention or intention on the line, or to produce (create) an effect.

**ZU** : the ancient Sumerian cuneiform sign for the archaic verb—*"to know," "knowingness"* or *"awareness"*; in *Mardukite Zuism and Systemology*, the active energy/matter of the "Spiritual Universe" (AN) experienced as a *Lifeforce* or *consciousness* that imbues living forms extant in the "Physical Universe" (KI); *"Spiritual Life Energy"*; energy demonstrated by the WILL of an actualized *Alpha-Spirit* in the "Spiritual Universe" (AN), which impinges its *Awareness* into the Physical Universe (KI), animating/controlling *Life* for its experience of *beta-existence* along an individual Alpha-Spirit's personal *Identity-continuum*, called a *ZU-line*.

**Zu-Line** : a theoretical construct in *Mardukite Zuism and Systemology* demonstrating *Spiritual*

*Life Energy* (*ZU*) as a personal individual "continuum" of Awareness interacting with all Spheres of Existence on the Standard Model of Systemology; a spectrum of potential variations and interactions of a monistic continuum or singular *Spiritual Life Energy* demonstrated on the Standard Model; an energetic channel of potential POV and "locations" of Beingness, demonstrated in early Systemology materials as an individual Alpha-Spirit's personal *Identity- continuum*, potentially connecting *Awareness* of *Self* with "*Infinity*" simultaneous with all points considered in existence; a symbolic demonstration of the "*Life-line*" on which *Awareness (ZU)* extends from the direction of the "Spiritual Universe" (AN) in its true original *alpha state* through an entire possible range of activity resulting in its *beta state* and control of a *genetic-entity* occupying the *Physical Universe (KI).*

**Zu**-**Vision** : the true and basic (*Alpha*) Point-of-View (perspective, POV) maintained by *Self* as *Alpha-Spirit* outside boundaries or considerations of the *Human Condition* and *exterior* to beta-existence reality agreements with the Physical Universe; a POV of Self *as* "a unit of Spiritual Awareness" that exists independent of a "body" and entrapment in a *Human Condition*; "spirit vision" in its truest sense.

*explore the*
## Fundamentals of Systemology

All *six*
Basic Course
lesson booklets
*in one*
hardcover
edition!

*start your journey on the*
## The Pathway to Ascension

All *sixteen*
Professional Course
lesson booklets
*in two*
hardcover
volumes!

# THE SYSTEMOL

Seekers and students of the *Basic Course* and *Professional Course* will also be interested in the *Systemology Core Research Series*. These eight volumes are a complete chronological record of the Mardukite New Thought developments from the Systemology Society, published in 2019 through 2023.

The *Systemology Core* begins with the first professional publication released when the *Mardukite Systemology Society* emerged from the underground in 2019, with: *"The Tablets of Destiny Revelation."*

# OGY PATHWAY

PUBLISHED BY THE **JOSHUA FREE** IMPRINT REPRESENTING

**The Mardukite Academy of Systemology**

THE JOSHUA FREE IMPRINT
JFI PUBLICATIONS

MARDUKITE
ZUISM

**mardukite.com**

www.ingramcontent.com/pod-product-compliance
Lightning Source LLC
Chambersburg PA
CBHW071211120626
46546CB00006B/2509